U.S. Department of Justice
Office of Justice Programs
National Institute of Justice

JUNE 06

I0475780

NIJ

Special **REPORT**

Drug Courts: The Second Decade

www.ojp.usdoj.gov/nij

U.S. Department of Justice
Office of Justice Programs
810 Seventh Street N.W.
Washington, DC 20531

Alberto R. Gonzales
Attorney General

Regina B. Schofield
Assistant Attorney General

Glenn R. Schmitt
Acting Director, National Institute of Justice

This and other publications and products of the National Institute
of Justice can be found at:

National Institute of Justice
www.ojp.usdoj.gov/nij

Office of Justice Programs
Partnerships for Safer Communities
www.ojp.usdoj.gov

JUNE 06

Drug Courts: The Second Decade

NCJ 211081□

Glenn R. Schmitt
Acting Director

Findings and conclusions of the research reported here are those of the author(s) and do not necessarily reflect the official position or policies of the U.S. Department of Justice.

The National Institute of Justice is a component of the Office of Justice Programs, which also includes the Bureau of Justice Assistance, the Bureau of Justice Statistics, the Office of Juvenile Justice and Delinquency Prevention, and the Office for Victims of Crime.

About This Report

Researchers have begun to look at the inner workings of drug courts and to investigate how key functional drug court components, singly and in combination, affect outcomes. When the evidence base resulting from such research is sufficiently strong to support meaningful conclusions about effectiveness, research can be translated into practice.

This compendium presents findings from several recent studies that speak to the concerns of practitioners and policymakers about "what works." Sometimes the studies confirm what previous research has found, and sometimes they raise more questions than they answer. But in every instance, they contribute to the slowly building base of knowledge about "the drug court effect."

What did the researchers find?

- Research indicates that drug courts can reduce recidivism and promote other positive outcomes. However, research has not uncovered which court processes affect which outcomes and for what types of offenders. The magnitude of a court's impact may depend upon how consistently court resources match the needs of the offenders in the drug court program.

- To address alcohol and drug problems, treatment services should (1) be based on formal theories of drug dependence and abuse, (2) use the best therapeutic tools, and (3) give participants opportunities to build cognitive skills. Treatment that applies a scattershot approach— of sometimes incompatible philosophies—may be counterproductive.

In addition, ancillary services that address co-occurring mental and physical health, housing, and other needs may be helpful.

- Compared to adults, juveniles can be difficult to diagnose and treat. Many young people referred to drug court have no established pattern of abuse or physical addiction. Others have reached serious levels of criminal and drug involvement. Neither general treatment research nor drug court evaluations have produced definitive information on juveniles. Most juvenile drug court teams are still exploring whether their mission should be prevention or intervention.

- Proper assessment and treatment of offenders is primarily the responsibility of service providers, but all drug court team members should be concerned with the integrity of treatment planning, service delivery, and performance reporting (including drug test results). Teams that are educated in addiction and substance abuse theory, treatment approaches, and relapse prevention are better able to ensure that offender needs are met.

- Offenders report that interactions with the judge are one of the most important influences on the experience they have while in the program. They respond to the judge's interpersonal skills and ability to resolve legal problems expeditiously and provide ready access to services. Offenders who interact with a single drug court judge, rather than multiple judges, may be more likely to comply with program demands.

- Programs are influenced by a variety of factors that may be external (e.g., trends in drug use), internal (e.g., staff turnover), or policy-related (e.g., diversion versus post-disposition). Because the impact of these factors may change over time, studying a court over several years offers feedback on how past policies and procedures affect program outcomes.

■ The decision to allocate resources to a drug court should be based on a demon-strated benefit (such as reduced recidi-vism) given the costs and savings. Drug courts can estimate costs using figures found in public information sources (i.e., proxies like the average cost of incarcer-ation). More definitive analyses examine costs incurred by every agency involved. One definitive cost-benefit evaluation estimated the average investment per program participant was $5,928; the savings were $2,329 in avoided criminal justice system costs and $1,301 in avoided victimization costs over a 30-month period.

What were the studies' limitations?

The specific limitations for each study are noted in the relevant chapters. But all of the studies were hindered by the lack of accessible data on many aspects of drug court operations. Adequate data systems are essential to support research and to link the core components of the program to recidivism and other outcomes.

DRUG COURTS: THE SECOND DECADE SYNTHESIZES SELECTED FINDINGS FROM THE NIJ-FUNDED RESEARCH LISTED BELOW:

■ Anspach, Donald F., and Andrew S. Ferguson. "Assessing the Efficacy of Treatment Modalities in the Context of Adult Drug Courts, Final Report." Grant No. 2000–DC–VX–0008.

■ Butts, Jeffrey A., and John Roman, eds. *Juvenile Drug Courts and Teen Substance Abuse*. Washington, DC: The Urban Institute Press, 2004. (Based on research conducted under Grant No. 2000–DC–VX–K003).

■ Carey, Shannon M., and Michael W. Finigan. "Detailed Cost Analysis in a Mature Drug Court Setting: A Cost-Benefit Evaluation of the Multnomah County Drug Court." Grant No. 2000–DC–VX–K004.

■ Finigan, Michael W., and Shannon M. Carey. "Analysis of 26 Drug Courts: Lessons Learned, Final Report." (Commissioned paper, 2002).

■ Goldkamp, John S., Michael D. White, and Jennifer B. Robinson. "From Whether to How Drug Courts Work: Retrospective Evaluation of Two Pioneering Drug Courts in Clark County (Las Vegas) and Multnomah County (Portland), Phase II Report from the National Evaluation of Drug Courts." Grant No. 98–DC–VX–K001.

Contents

About This Report iii

Overview of Drug Courts. 1

Target Populations, Participant Attributes, and Program Outcomes:
The Clark County Experience 5

The Judge's Role in Drug Court Participants' Success 9

Treatment Issues in the Drug Court Setting. 13

Drug Court Intervention for Juveniles 21

Cost-Benefit Analysis of a Mature Drug Court. 27

Overview of Drug Courts

Drug courts merge competing perspectives on the causes of substance abuse and addiction. The criminal justice model views drug addiction as one of many anti-social behaviors manifested by criminals, whereas the medical model views it as a chronic and relapsing disease. Traditionally, the courts use legal sanctions, including incarceration, both to punish drug-involved offenders and to deter them from further criminal activity. On the other hand, the treatment community emphasizes therapeutic relationships to help motivate addicts to reduce their dependence on drugs, change their behavior, and take control of their lives.

Drug courts offer an alternative to incarceration, which, by itself, has not been effective in breaking the cycle of drugs and crime. Treatment has been shown to work—if substance abusers stick with it; however, between 80 and 90 percent of conventional drug treatment clients drop out before 12 months, the period generally found to be the minimum effective duration.[1] By providing a structure that links supervision and treatment, drug courts exert legal pressure on defendants to enter and remain in treatment long enough to realize benefits. More than two-thirds of participants who begin treatment through a drug court complete it in a year or more—a sixfold increase in retention compared with programs outside the justice system.[2]

Drug courts emerged in the late 1980s in response to rapidly increasing felony drug caseloads that strained the Nation's courts and overflowed its jails and prisons. The first drug court was established in Miami, Florida, in 1989, with the goal of reducing substance abuse and criminal behavior while also freeing the court and corrections systems to handle other cases. Since then, the Office of Justice Programs (OJP) has awarded millions of dollars to fund drug courts. As of December 2005, more than 1,500 drug courts were operating and another 391 were being planned.[3]

According to the National Institute of Drug Abuse (NIDA), involuntary treatment can be effective.[4] Of the thousands of offenders who have participated in the courts since 1989, it is fair to say that most would not have entered treatment by choice. Drug courts have coerced an impressive number of substance-involved offenders—many of whom have co-occurring mental, emotional, and physical health problems—to receive treatment, counseling, and other services that they need if they are to lead productive and law-abiding lives. In some communities, drug use is now the major vector for the spread of HIV/AIDS, tuberculosis, and hepatitis C. The drug court movement thus has great potential for improving both public safety and public health. In fact, the *National Drug Control Strategy Update,* issued in March 2004 by the White House, hailed the creation of drug courts as "one of the most promising trends in the criminal justice system."[5]

Lessons Learned About Implementation

In analyzing the processes of 26 drug courts, researchers identified several obstacles to smooth program functioning that administrators frequently encounter and recommended ways to deal with them:

■ Developing an effective management information system—the top priority for drug court administrators—and doing it at the earliest stages of planning.

■ Accurately estimating the drug court's enrollment population through a clearly delineated referral process, sufficiently strict eligibility requirements (to ensure that only appropriate offenders are admitted), and built-in incentives (to make enrollment worth the difficulty of completing the program).

■ Spending the time and resources necessary to gain genuine "buy-in" among collaborating line staff and developing clear and specific protocols for cooperation among key stakeholders.

■ Adhering to a balanced system of sanctions and rewards that can be applied consistently and appropriately in response to participant behaviors.

■ Establishing well-defined written protocols on program processes to ensure the quality and consistent delivery of services (and building awareness of how deviation from these protocols can impede success).

■ Thoroughly researching any contemplated services and realistically assessing what can be accomplished within budget parameters.

■ "Institutionalizing" the court from the very beginning so that changes in key personnel do not undermine program integrity.

■ Carefully defining the conditions that must be met in each step of a treatment phase before a participant can move on to the next one. The transition should be based on compliance with the treatment regimen, which indicates progress toward goals.

■ Maintaining responsibility for the screening and assessment of referrals within the court. Transferring assessment to the treatment provider may save money, but it reduces the amount of data the court can collect on its referral process and target population— information that is vital to understanding the risk level of participants and evaluating program effectiveness.

■ Finding a reliable provider of timely urinalysis results—necessary to ensure that sanctions for substance abuse are imposed swiftly and certainly—or hiring staff and purchasing the needed equipment to perform the tests within the program.

■ Preventing absconding by providing participants with incentives to remain in the program.

Based on a report funded by the National Institute of Justice in 2001 and prepared by Michael W. Finigan and Shannon M. Carey of NPC Research, Inc., in Portland, Oregon. The report, "Analysis of 26 Drug Courts: Lessons Learned, Final Report," (2002) is available online at www.ncjrs.org.pdffiles1/nij/grants/194046.pdf.

Types of drug courts

Communities have shaped their drug court programs to fit local circumstances such as the prevailing drug-use and drug-arrest patterns, the availability of treatment resources and ancillary services, and public opinion about being "tough on crime." Courts may be based on diversion, pretrial/presentence, postadjudication, or probation revocation strategies, in which the judge exercises authority to defer case disposition if a defendant agrees to participate in drug court. On successful completion of the program, case processing may end with dropped charges, vacated or reduced sentences, or rescinded probation. Increasingly courts have moved from targeting low-level and first-time offenders to focusing on those whose substance abuse and criminal activity may be more serious and pose a greater threat to society—and a greater challenge to drug courts. When taking on such high-risk

The Drug Court Model

In January 1997, the National Association of Drug Court Professionals and the U.S. Department of Justice's Office of Justice Programs published *Defining Drug Courts: The Key Components,* which describes the basic elements that define drug courts and offers performance benchmarks to guide implementation. The 10 key components are:

- Integration of substance abuse treatment with justice system case processing.

- Use of a nonadversarial approach, in which prosecution and defense promote public safety while protecting the right of the accused to due process.

- Early identification and prompt placement of eligible participants.

- Access to a continuum of treatment, rehabilitation, and related services.

- Frequent testing for alcohol and illicit drugs.

- A coordinated strategy among the judge, prosecution, defense, and treatment providers to govern offender compliance.

- Ongoing judicial interaction with each participant.

- Monitoring and evaluation to measure achievement of program goals and gauge effectiveness.

- Continuing interdisciplinary education to promote effective planning, implementation, and operation.

- Partnerships with public agencies and community-based organizations to generate local support and enhance drug court effectiveness.

---

offenders, drug court personnel need to understand that addiction is a health problem that is difficult to cure and requires long-term treatment. Relapses may be frequent, making it necessary to extend treatment well beyond the typical 12-month period.

Despite the differences in drug courts from jurisdiction to jurisdiction, most face common implementation problems (see "Lessons Learned About Implementation"). And almost all drug courts share the elements and adhere to the principles outlined in *Defining Drug Courts: The Key Components,* a report produced by a group of drug court practitioners convened by the National Association of Drug Court Professionals and funded by the former Drug Courts Program Office within OJP (see "The Drug Court Model"). Although widely known as "the drug court model," the components listed in the report are not theory based and have not been linked by evidence to program outcomes. Nevertheless, they provide sound guid-

ance for developing a drug court and offer measurable performance benchmarks that are useful to researchers.

Evaluating drug court effectiveness and impact

Critics have faulted drug court evaluations overall for their lack of scientific rigor, but a number of randomized and controlled experimental studies published in peer-reviewed journals have found that drug court graduates have significantly lower rearrest rates—lasting more than 2 years beyond graduation—than those who do not participate in the program. In addition, researchers are beginning to isolate the effects of the various "key components" of drug courts in order to establish their efficacy.

The National Institute of Justice has funded a multisite evaluation of adult drug courts that builds on previous studies.

The evaluation is measuring the impact of drug courts in rural, suburban, and urban sites using a novel research design that factors in the characteristics of the community, the court, and the offender. The researchers are examining the influence of court programs on recidivism, use of treatment and ancillary services, use of drugs and alcohol, and other behavior changes such as employment.

Notes

1. Huddleston, C. West, Karen Freeman-Wilson, and Donna L. Boone, *Painting the Current Picture: A National Report Card on Drug Courts and Other Problem Solving Court Programs in the United States*, Alexandria, VA: National Drug Court Institute, May 2004.

2. Ibid.

3. The American University Drug Court Clearinghouse and the Bureau of Justice Assistance's Technical Assistance Project reported 1,550 drug courts in operation in December 2005. Of these, 937 were adult courts, 385 were juvenile courts, 164 were family courts, and 58 were tribal courts. (Visit the clearinghouse at www.spa.american.edu/justice/drugcourts.php.)

4. Principle 10 from "The Thirteen Principles of Effective Drug Addiction Treatment" available online at www.nida.nih.gov/NIDA_Notes/NNVol14N5/tearoff.html.

5. The White House, *National Drug Control Strategy, Update*, March 2004, Washington, DC: The White House, available online at http://www.state.gov/documents/organization/30228.pdf.

Target Populations, Participant Attributes, and Program Outcomes: The Clark County Experience

Many factors affect a drug court's decision about what type of offender to allow into the treatment program. Law enforcement strategies, prosecutor practices, and probation and parole policies figure prominently in such decisions, as do other external factors such as the availability of treatment and service providers in the community, the "buy-in" of elected officials, and the safety concerns of the general public. These considerations may influence drug courts to target a particular population in response to a perceived need (e.g., high arrest rates for methamphetamine use) or a chronic problem (e.g., overcrowding in local jails).

Targeting decisions require careful planning because they have an impact on every aspect of drug court operations—from eligibility and screening determinations to delivery of treatment and service options to sanctions for noncompliance. They also affect "success" rates; different types of offenders bring different needs and risk levels to the program. Drug courts handling high-need, high-risk offenders are likely to have lower graduation rates and higher rearrest rates than those targeting minor or first-time offenders, so court planners must ground their expectations in reality.

An evaluation of the Clark County (Las Vegas) Drug Court demonstrates that factors outside the control of the drug court—especially a shift from diversion to conviction-based entry requirements—changed the characteristics of the target population, which, in turn, had substantial impact on the drug court's effectiveness.[1]

Drug court enrollment and participant attributes

The research was designed to capture the effects of important changes in the drug court from 1993 to 1997—including changes in targeted and enrolled populations—by studying cohorts of defendants who entered the drug court in successive time periods. Collecting data about screening and enrollment revealed trends that give a rough indication of the jurisdiction's success in establishing a program that reaches its target population; in addition, trends in the enrollment and volume of participants admitted over time have significant implications for program performance and vitality in other areas.

The research team looked at external factors and events that may have played a major role in defining the type of defendants to participate in the drug court. An analysis of trends in drug arrests during the periods studied found nothing to indicate that drug court screening and enrollment were merely a reflection of drug arrests produced through local law enforcement activities. When researchers analyzed milestones in the court's implementation history, however, they found that impacts on enrollment were associated with several factors outside the drug court (see "Milestones in the Implementation of the Clark County Drug Court").

After the prosecutor decided that offenders must plead guilty to enter drug court, the percentage of defendants choosing to enroll increased, but the actual number of enrollees dropped. Fewer eligible defendants were willing to consider drug court

because they could no longer avoid conviction. Other external factors caused an increase in enrollment:

- Enactment of a law allowing probation, rather than prison, for drug felonies made the drug court option more attractive to the district attorney, who viewed it as more intensive and effective than simple probation and began referring more cases to the drug court.

- A court order requiring offenders to appear in court within 48 hours of their arrest reduced the number of offenders held in the county detention center before trial by placing pressure on the court system to make greater use of early disposition options and/or to resolve detainees' cases more promptly.

Target changes affect participant attributes . . .

In general, variations in enrollment from court to court reflect local drug use patterns as well as local law enforcement strategies. The shift in Clark County's prosecutorial policy changed both the number and the characteristics of drug court enrollees. Increasingly, the court enrolled offenders convicted of drug-related crimes, such as burglary (up from 9 percent in 1993 to 18 percent in 1997). The average age of participants increased from 28 years at the beginning of the study period to 31 years at the study's end. Female participants dropped from 38 percent initially to 24 percent in 1997. The proportion of participants who were black grew from 9 percent in 1993 to 27 percent in 1997. In 1993 and 1994, approximately 78 percent of participants were white (larger than the white proportion of the overall court caseload), whereas in 1995–97, the proportion dropped to 60 percent.

Drug use patterns, which were recorded at initial assessment, did not vary notably over the 5–year study period, although

they differed markedly along racial and ethnic lines. On entering the program, blacks and Hispanics reported two to three times the use of cocaine as white participants, who more frequently reported methamphetamine abuse (from one-half to two-thirds of white participants, depending on the year). Methamphetamine use was much less common among Hispanic participants and nearly nonexistent among blacks.

. . . and participant behavior

This higher risk participant profile was related to an increased use of jail time as a sanction for noncompliance with program requirements. Overall, 35 percent of Clark County Drug Court participants were confined at least once because they failed to comply over 2 years from the date they entered drug court. However, the overall rate masks a remarkable increase over time; from 1993 to 1995, 21 percent were sent to jail, whereas from 1995 to 1997, 51 percent were sent to jail. The average time spent in confinement as a result of sanctions also increased over the years studied, as the court shifted to admitting convicted offenders. Based on the 2-year followup, participants during the study period overall (1993–97) spent, on average, no time in jail. But jail time ranged from an average of 0 days among the 1993–95 participants to an average of 5 days among 1996 participants and 13 days among the 1997 group.

When only those who were confined are examined (rather than the whole group, some of whom were never confined), the increasing trend can be seen more clearly. The average number of jail days jumped from 6 among the 1993 participants to 13 among the 1995 participants and 22 among the 1997 participants—a more than

threefold increase. Researchers attributed the increased use of jail as a sanction to the changed nature of the caseload and the higher risk of noncompliance and reoffending it represented rather than to a change in the sanctioning philosophy of the court judge.

The study team analyzed how the number and type of sanctions received related to the likelihood of rearrest 1 year after drug court admission and graduation within 2 years. In Clark County, imposing *any* sanction was associated with higher rearrest and lower graduation rates. These findings show that drug court participants may leave clues about higher risk during their time in treatment; thus, additional supervision or services for clients who are sanctioned early in the program may help reduce later recidivism and dropout.

Short-term recidivism

Overall, drug court participants from 1993 through 1997 were rearrested (for any charge) less often than their counterparts in the comparison group (randomly selected from all felony drug cases that did not enter drug court): 53 percent versus 65 percent, respectively. But the rearrest rate was actually higher for the 1996 drug court admissions cohort (73 percent compared to 65 percent for the comparison group) and was only slightly lower (56 percent) than the comparison group (59 percent) in 1997. Again, these findings correspond to the shift from a diversion-based to a conviction-based population of participants. External factors such as this one may have substantial impacts on a drug court's effectiveness. Researchers are advised to monitor both internal and external factors during drug court evaluations to avoid misinterpreting patterns in participant outcomes.

Note

1. The information in this chapter was obtained from the second phase of a study funded by NIJ under grant number 98–DC–VX–K001 to evaluate two of the Nation's oldest drug courts. Researchers from Temple University's Crime and Research Institute—John S. Goldkamp, Michael D. White, and Jennifer B. Robinson—submitted "From Whether to How Drug Courts Work: Retrospective Evaluation of Two Pioneering Drug Courts in Clark County (Las Vegas) and Multnomah County (Portland), Phase II Report from the National Evaluation of Drug Courts" in 2002. The full report can be viewed online at www.ncjrs.org/pdffiles1/nij/grants/194124.pdf.

The Judge's Role in Drug Court Participants' Success

The drug court model identifies the judge's role as key to program success. The model presumes that effectiveness depends on the judge's nontraditional style (informal, hands-on, and flexible), the nonadversarial nature of proceedings, the frequency of required hearings, and the opportunity for direct communication between defendants and the bench. However, none of these presumptions has been tested.

A study of the Multnomah County Drug Court in Portland, Oregon, examined key functional program elements of the drug court intervention (such as status hearings drug testing, treatment, and sanctions) to determine their relative contributions, over time, to the impact of drug courts (i.e., the "drug court effect").[1] Researchers investigated presumptions of the drug court model, including whether dedication of a single judge to the drug court's effort is necessary for success.

Examining the single-judge hypothesis

A single dedicated judge presided over the Multnomah County Drug Court from its inception in 1991 through 1995; in January 1996, the court began an experiment using a referee—a quasi-judicial officer who functioned as a judge but had fewer powers. This innovation was followed in 1997 by the assignment of a mix of 16 judges and referees to serve on a rotating basis for relatively short intervals (a change that drug court advocates would argue was a serious dilution of the drug court model). At about the same time that the court switched to using referees, it also implemented standards specifying conditions for mandatory program termination.

Automatic early termination policies, adopted in 1994, required that offenders who do not participate in treatment for an extended period of time (up to a year)—because of bench warrant status or program suspension—be dropped summarily. By 1996 the court had adopted a rule to automatically terminate participants on bench warrant status for 3 consecutive months. The court's many changes in judicial oversight during the study period (1991–97) offered an unusual opportunity to look at assumptions about the accuracy of the "one judge" hypothesis; specifically, researchers examined whether differences in judicial staffing were related to participant outcomes. They found that 90 percent of offenders who entered the drug court program between 1991 and 1995 experienced only one or two judges presiding over their court appearances. However, 10 percent (most of whom entered the program in 1995) were exposed to three to five judges. After 1995, participant exposure to multiple judges shifted dramatically. Approximately one-fourth of participants entering in 1996 and 1997 were exposed to one or two judges, about one-half experienced three to five judges (or referees), and another one-fourth were exposed to six or more.

Findings about the judge's role

Researchers assumed that the drug court model, which presumes an important effect associated with the single judge, would predict that participants supervised in court by one or two judges would have much better outcomes than those

supervised by many judges. Supposedly, the latter group would not feel personally connected to the judge and would receive inconsistent treatment from session to session with regard to the handling of noncompliance. Analyses of tests to determine rates of reoffending, however, produced surprising and equivocal findings (see "Study Methods"). Those exposed to five or more judges had the *lowest* probability of rearrest compared to other groups, while those exposed to only one judge produced the next lowest rearrest rate. Researchers believe that the shift toward greater use of automatic early termination policies influenced rearrest outcomes—in conjunction with, or independent of, the move in 1996 toward referees and frequent rotation.

Further analyses of different outcome measures (appearances before the court, for example) suggest that, whether or not "judge exposure" plays a first-order role in shaping outcomes, it is clearly tied to other time-related factors, such as length of treatment. Researchers found that the more judges participants saw, the greater their likelihood of poor treatment attendance—a finding that may be significant if, in fact, increased retention in treatment (the principal rationale for the judge's hands-on supervision) increases the chances of better outcomes in general.

In addition, judge exposure also seemed to influence unfavorable termination (i.e., the more judges seen per 100 days, the greater the likelihood of early termination). Offenders who took part in the program during the years when a single dedicated judge presided in the courtroom were far less likely to be terminated early and far more likely to miss fewer than five treatment sessions than those enrolled when multiple judges or referees presided in rotation.

Finally, when researchers considered judge exposure along with length of treatment, they found that exposure to multiple judges predicted rearrest for nondrug offenses (but not for rearrest of any type).

In focus group sessions with drug court participants, offenders told researchers that personal attention from the judge during status hearings (which take up the greatest portion, by far, of a drug court judge's time) was the most important influence in their drug court experience. This special relationship, along with the judge's ability to resolve issues involving old warrants, childcare, employment, and social services, was pivotal in keeping participants in the program.

Implications for further research

Researchers found evidence both to support and not to support the importance of the single-judge approach, depending on the outcome that was examined. They speculate that the single-judge hypothesis might actually represent other presumptions of the drug court model, such as the need for effective judicial supervision, continuity of monitoring, and consistency in rules and responses to participant behavior during the drug court process. Additional studies are currently being conducted to specifically test the impact of judicial oversight.

Note

1. The information in this chapter was obtained from the second phase of a study funded by NIJ under grant number 98–DC–VX–K001 to evaluate two of the Nation's oldest drug courts. Researchers from Temple University's Crime and Justice Research Institute—John S. Goldkamp, Michael D. White, and Jennifer B. Robinson—submitted "From Whether to How Drug Courts Work: Retrospective Evaluation of Two Pioneering Drug Courts in Clark County (Las Vegas) and Multnomah County (Portland), Phase II Report from the National Evaluation of Drug Courts" in 2002. The full report is available online at www.ncjrs.org/pdffiles1/nij/grants/194124.pdf.

Treatment Issues in the Drug Court Setting

Court-supervised treatment is at the heart of the drug court model, which presumes that changing the drug-using habits of offenders will reduce both criminal behavior and addiction. Findings from a study of four well-established "mentor" drug courts (see "Structure of the Four Drug Courts") show that they are moving toward these dual goals.[1] The research confirms what other studies have found: Drug court graduates succeed and terminated participants fail, indicating that administrators should continue to focus on improvements in program retention and completion rates. But the study also identified weaknesses and deficiencies—especially in terms of treatment quality and delivery, program integration and integrity, and other implementation issues—that suggest drug courts have yet to reach their full potential.

Treatment delivery and quality

Three of the four drug courts studied obtained substance abuse treatment services directly through dedicated providers with whom they had some formal agreement. Only the Bakersfield, California, drug court used multiple external treatment providers, assigning drug court clients to dedicated slots located close to their residence. Overall, the four sites provided access to drug treatment services that are similar to those identified as available in a national survey of drug courts.[2] Across the board, however, these jurisdictions did not

offer treatment services that represent the standard of highly individualized care called for in the drug court model.

Continuum of care

Each drug court tried to provide access to a continuum of alcohol, drug, and other related treatment and rehabilitation services. Except for the residential program in Jackson County, Missouri, the programs referred clients to other agencies for medical services. Although treatment providers cannot be expected to provide such services to a population that is likely to have multiple co-occurring medical issues, the ability to do so is no doubt a benefit.

Services for specific groups—the hearing and sight impaired and Spanish speakers—were not offered "in house" by the study sites, and none provided a specifically designed postgraduation aftercare program. In addition, researchers found that treatment programs lacked formal cooperative agreements with external providers of ancillary services (such as assistance with education, vocational training, transportation, and housing), relying instead on informal referral systems. Nothing at any site indicated that direct providers are substantively involved in ensuring that participants receive services for which they are referred.

To the extent that participants in the four programs have an array of social, interpersonal, and psychological needs, the

STRUCTURE OF THE FOUR DRUG COURTS

Researchers examined the treatment programs and operations of drug courts in Bakersfield, California; Creek County, Oklahoma; Jackson County, Missouri; and St. Mary Parish, Louisiana. These courts adopted the general features of the drug court model to fit particular local needs. As shown below, some basic elements are common to all sites, but the four programs differ in ways that affect the selection and processing of cases.

For example, all four programs offer a stepdown phased system of requirements, meaning that, as participants progress through program phases, both treatment and court requirements decrease. Stepdown requirements vary by site, except that all require attendance at treatment sessions and status hearings as well as participation in drug testing.

Drug Court Structure	Bakersfield Postplea, Postadjudication	Creek County Postplea, Postadjudication	Jackson County Preplea, Preadjudication	St. Mary Parish Postplea, Predjudication
Differentiated Program Levels or Tracks*	One	2 Drug Court Tracks 4 Treatment Tracks	6 Treatment Tracks	One
Phase I	4 months	3 months	4 months	2 months
Phase II	4 months	3 months	4 months	4 months
Phase III	4 months	3 months	4 months	3 months
Phase IV	NA	3 months	NA	6 months
Program Length**	12 months	12 months	12 months	15 months
Date of Inception	1993	1997	1993	1997
Target Population	DUI/DWI and misdemeanor offenders only	Felony and misdemeanor offenders	Felony and misdemeanor offenders	Felony and misdemeanor offenders

* Does not include participants placed in residential treatment.
** Program and phase lengths reflect minimum timeframes for completion.

reliance on informal referral systems may hamper the ability of drug courts to effectively provide the entire range of services necessary for the high-need, high-risk criminal justice populations they serve.

Treatment program staff

Drug treatment program staff at the four drug courts had relatively low levels of education, although some had professional licenses or certifications. A number of counselors were recovering substance abusers themselves. The programs

employed comparatively few case managers, suggesting that responsibility for activities such as transitional planning and referral to social services may be pushed onto clinical staff—or not given sufficient priority.

In addition, the sites had few minority counselors, despite the fact that many of them served a fairly large number of minority offenders. Counselors worked 30 to 40 hours per week and conducted three to six group sessions, totaling 6 to 8 hours, per week. Each group had about

STUDY METHODS

This study was designed to examine the delivery of treatment services in four drug courts. It involved a retrospective analysis of the impact of functional drug court components on offender outcomes, both during program participation and during a 1-year postprogram followup period.

The study used both qualitative and quantitative analyses of information. Fieldwork consisted of:

- Onsite interviews conducted with key court and treatment stakeholders.

- Surveys of 52 treatment counselors (58 percent response rate).

- Observations of 124 treatment sessions, which were assessed using a structured tool designed to measure the nature and quality of various clinical components of substance abuse treatment.

For the retrospective study, the researchers used regression models to analyze the records of 2,357 offenders enrolled in the four drug courts between 1997 and 2000. They tested (1) the combined effect of participant characteristics and program compliance measures on drug court graduation, and (2) the relationship of four variables (participant characteristics, measures of program compliance, discharge status, and time at risk [exposure]) to the likelihood of postprogram rearrest. Arrest data were obtained from the National Crime Information Center. Other data were obtained from a variety of community sources, including courts and the treatment providers.

Researchers noted three limitations to the research: (1) The retrospective and exploratory components used different cohorts; that is, the participants whose records were examined in the retrospective study were different from those enrolled in the program during the exploratory component of the study. (2) Data on status hearings and sanctions were very limited or unavailable. (3) No data were available on the offenders who were determined to be eligible for the program but chose not to participate; therefore, a comparison of participants and nonparticipants was not possible.

10 to 15 clients. Counselors spent, on average, 41 percent of their time in counseling and the rest on administrative tasks. Caseloads ranged from 25 to 75 clients, depending on the site. Most of the counselors interviewed attributed addiction to personality characteristics and individual experience rather than to social influences.

Therapeutic approaches

Staff survey results indicate that treatment counselors were willing to use any tools or techniques that had a chance of working, and direct observation of treatment activities confirmed this claim (see "Study Methods"). Counselors used a number of approaches concurrently, with little indepth focus on any particular therapeutic issue. Only the Creek County drug court had a formal curriculum, which researchers considered essential to effective rehabilitation.

Although a mixed approach to substance abuse treatment may sound like an effective way to address multiple participant needs, these programs, in fact, lacked coherence and were based on incompatible philosophies. For example, considerable time was spent on increasing participants' awareness of possible "triggers" leading to renewed drug use, yet information on what to do with this knowledge was inadequate; i.e., preventing a relapse was not sufficiently emphasized. In part, this was so because counselors

were trying several other treatment approaches at the same time, with the result that messages to participants were often inconsistent.

The 12-step approach, which advocates that participants recognize they lack the strength or resources to control their addiction and turn their lives over to a higher power, was sometimes coupled with cognitive-behavioral therapy (CBT) techniques. CBT requires participants to recognize and examine the role played by thoughts and emotions in perpetuating addictive behavior and take control of internal processes by learning new social, emotional, and cognitive skills. The two approaches work against each other in terms of their underlying views of the origins of substance abuse. CBT, considered to be one of the most effective approaches to substance abuse treatment, was used in only about 22 percent of the counseling sessions observed; when offered at all, CBT was allocated from 8 to 26 minutes.

None of the programs was founded on a formal theory of the causes of drug dependence, nor did any articulate a policy about the best therapeutic tools to use. Researchers believe that the lack of a theory-based approach to treatment and the dearth of cognitive skill-building opportunities may have resulted in treatment that was less intensive than needed to address the chronic, relapsing nature of drug addiction.

Observers cited other treatment deficiencies, including very limited inclusion of family members in counseling sessions. The assistance of family is needed to help offender-addicts lead "clean" lives—a matter of particular importance to the participants in these drug courts, most of whom lived in the community during

treatment. In addition, the sites offered little in the way of gender- or culture-specific programming. Although the majority of participants at most sites were white males, each jurisdiction served substantial minority and female populations who would have benefited from services tailored to their specific needs.

Integration of court operations and treatment services

How well have drug courts been able to integrate court operations and treatment services in terms of philosophy, policy development/decisionmaking, information sharing, and staff familiarity with cross-program issues? Philosophically, treatment and court staff at the four sites share similar views about the role substance abuse plays in criminal behavior and the priority accorded treatment in the drug court program. Both groups believe substance abuse is related to and precedes criminal behavior, that coerced treatment is effective, and that treatment delivery is the primary goal of the drug court program.

At the operational level, the programs rely on several common mechanisms to enhance collaboration among treatment and court staff:

- Combined court and treatment requirements for participants in the stepdown phased system.

- Institutionalized lines of communication through weekly precourt meetings in which court and treatment staff discuss participant progress.

- Representation from both groups on steering committees and other decisionmaking and policy bodies.

However, criminal justice staff have limited knowledge of the techniques and realistic goals of substance abuse treatment. Only a few court personnel reported attending treatment sessions, although treatment staff from all four sites were involved in drug court operations. At one site, court staff were unable to distinguish between the services delivered in "treatment" and those delivered in 12-step programs, even though they mandated participant attendance at both. In other words, court personnel were sending participants to services that they did not understand. As a result, court personnel may harbor unreasonable expectations about the degree of change likely to come from treatment and the length of time needed to achieve such change.

Several judges expressed an interest in attending treatment groups to better understand the process but felt that doing so might make participants uncomfortable. In light of these concerns, the researchers suggest that treatment staff periodically provide training sessions for court personnel to help them develop at least a basic understanding of the processes involved.

None of the courts had formal guidelines for administering sanctions or a system of graduated sanctions. Nor were records maintained on the types of sanctions imposed and the reasons for doing so. Improved integration of treatment and court procedures would allow sanctions to be tied to program compliance, as envisioned in the drug court model.

The drug court model calls for collaboration among various components of the criminal justice and substance abuse treatment systems to combine the coercive power of the court with effective and scientifically based treatment practices. With regard to achieving such collaboration in a truly integrated drug court, "best practices" have yet to be demonstrated, and little is known about the obstacles that stand in the way.

Program integrity

The drug court model aims to deliver an intervention that is structured, intensive, and demanding, so that as addict-offenders make progress in treatment, they become committed to recovery and are held accountable for their behavior. Ideally, an integrated program addresses the chronic nature of addiction through drug testing, sanctions, frequent status hearings, and substance abuse treatment. This study assessed the integrity of several core components of the programs at the four sites by comparing their protocols with actual drug court operations. An analysis of three program fidelity measures (length of program participation, drug testing compliance, and treatment attendance) revealed a number of gaps between intent and practice. The majority of drug court participants were not in compliance with one or more program requirements—an important fact because failure to comply with these requirements is related to unsuccessful completion of the program.

Program participation

Overall, 33 percent of offenders were active participants in drug court for longer than their respective program's scheduled length. Of these 33 percent who spent more than a year in the program, nearly one-fourth (23 percent) were terminated (expelled), indicating a possible net-widening problem. (Net widening occurs when a drug court broadens its eligibility and screening criteria to include individuals who are not appropriate for treatment.) The fact that 53 percent of total graduates participated beyond the expected program length also suggests that the standard 12-month timeframe may be too short to address the relapsing nature of addiction.

Treatment attendance and drug testing

Overall, 64 percent of participants did not attend a minimum number (70 percent) of the required treatment sessions. Findings also indicate that more than one-third of the participants (36.5 percent) graduated from drug court programs without having completed the minimum number of treatment sessions called for by program protocols.

In addition, the study found gaps between drug-testing requirements and actual drug-testing practices. More than half of all participants (54 percent) did not receive a minimum number of drug tests (70 percent) called for by the program's drug-testing requirements. A total of 33 percent of drug court graduates and 64 percent of terminated participants failed to meet the requirement. These results suggest that criminal justice supervision is too uneven to hold addicted offenders accountable for their behavior.

Taken together, the gaps between intent and practice in terms of program participation, treatment attendance, and drug testing indicate that the drug court intervention, as delivered, is not sufficiently intense—in treatment dosage or drug court oversight—to ensure either compliance or therapeutic progress.

Drug court participation and in-program recidivism

To attain the major goals of drug court programs—reducing criminal offending behaviors and substance abuse—

participants are required to comply with certain performance expectations, including avoiding new criminal conduct and abstaining from alcohol and drug use. Researchers examined how in-program recidivism and positive drug tests were related to program completion. Overall, the findings in this study indicate that 17 percent of participants were arrested once and 16 percent were arrested two or more times during their participation in drug court. In addition, 76 percent of participants tested positive for drug use one or more times, and 61 percent tested positive two or more times.

As expected, positive drug tests and in-program arrests are both negatively associated with program completion. A total of 85 percent of participants with in-program arrests and 50 percent of those with one or more positive drug tests were terminated from the program. In other words, terminated participants were two to three times more likely to test positive for drug use and four to five times more likely to be arrested during program participation than those who graduated.

Factors associated with postprogram recidivism

The overall "success" of drug court programs depends on whether offenders commit more crimes after they complete the program. Rearrest data for the 2,357 offenders in this study were obtained for 12 months past the date of discharge from the drug court program. As a result, researchers were able to examine the impact of compliance with program requirements on postprogram recidivism. Findings, shown in exhibit 1, confirm what other studies have found: Successful completion (graduation) of the drug court program is the variable most consistently associated with low postprogram recidivism.

Overall, 41 percent of the terminated participants and 9 percent of the graduates were rearrested. This means that, of the 722 participants in the postprogram followup who were rearrested, 90 percent had been expelled from their programs. The rate of postprogram recidivism is considerably higher for terminated participants than for graduates across all four sites. Moreover, terminated participants were rearrested in a shorter period of time—on average, 4.5 months after leaving the program—than graduates, whose rearrest took about 6.6 months.

Other factors associated with postprogram recidivism at one or more sites include:

■□**Treatment attendance.** Participants with low attendance at treatment sessions had a greater likelihood of being rearrested after program discharge.

■□**Race/ethnicity.** Members of racial and ethnic minority groups were more likely than non-Hispanic whites to be rearrested.

■□**Age at first arrest.** Participants with prior arrests at younger ages were more likely to be rearrested.

■□**Gender.** Males were more likely than females to be rearrested.

■□**In-program arrest.** Overall, participants with in-program arrests were twice as likely to have a postprogram rearrest. Among the 1,581 participants with no in-program arrests, 23 percent were rearrested after program discharge compared to 48 percent of the 776 participants with in-program arrests.

Exhibit 1. Postprogram rearrest outcomes in the four drug courts

	Bakersfield		Creek County		Jackson County		St. Mary Parish		Total	
	Grad.	Term.	Grad.	Term.	Grad.	Term.	Grad.	Term.	Grad.	Term.
Number of participants	261	462	93	99	354	868	70	150	778	1,579
With no rearrests	227	216	83	60	329	537	66	117	705	930
With one or more rearrests	34	246	10	39	25	331	4	33	73	649
Percent of total rearrests	12	88	20	80	7	93	11	89	10	90
Recidivism rates*										
Overall	38.7		25.5		29.1		16.8		30.6	
Graduates	13.0		10.8		7.1		5.7		9.4	
Terminations	53.2		39.4		38.1		22.0		41.1	

* Percent of program participants with postprogram rearrests.

Implications of this study

Findings from this study do not point to any defects in the drug court model itself. Instead, the research identifies deficiencies and problems in the way that treatment programs are delivered and suggests that drug courts may actually be shortchanging their clients in important respects. Although participants must bear some responsibility for failing to complete the program successfully, improvements are clearly needed in treatment content, access, and delivery; program integration; and program integrity so that drug courts can increase retention rates and achieve longer term reductions in drug use and criminal activity.

Notes

1. This chapter is based on an unpublished report by Donald F. Anspach, Ph.D., and Andrew S. Ferguson, "Assessing the Efficacy of Treatment Modalities in the Context of Adult Drug Courts, Final Report," prepared under grant number 2000–DC–VX–0008, which was awarded by NIJ to the University of Southern Maine. Available online at www.ncjrs.org/pdffiles1/nij/grants/202901.pdf.

2. Peyton, Elizabeth A., and Robert Gossweiler, *Treatment Services in Adult Drug Courts: Report on the 1999 National Drug Court Treatment Survey, Executive Summary.* Washington, DC: U.S. Department of Justice, Office of Justice Programs, Drug Courts Program Office, 2001.

Drug Court Intervention for Juveniles

Juvenile drug courts emerged during the mid-1990s as an alternative approach for dealing with young drug offenders. They have proliferated in the past decade, but most are still too new for researchers to determine whether they are effective. An NIJ-funded initiative to improve the methods available for evaluating juvenile drug court programs—the National Evaluation of Juvenile Drug Courts (NEJDC) project—raises several issues for consideration by juvenile justice practitioners and policymakers.[1]

Researchers are studying whether drug courts dedicated to juveniles are really necessary, since the traditional juvenile court already uses a problem-solving approach and recognizes the unique circumstances surrounding adolescent delinquency, including the use of alcohol and illicit drugs. Even if such a need can be established, they question the appropriateness of superimposing the adult model on youths whose criminal and drug-using profiles are markedly different from those of seriously addicted adult offenders. Finally, the study team discusses the apparent uncertainty of the juvenile drug court mission and asks officials to reflect on who should be eligible for these programs to ensure that limited resources yield the greatest good.

Adolescent drug use

National surveys of the general population report that almost all teenagers try alcohol or other drugs before they reach age 18. Although their rates of drug use substantially exceed those of adults, fewer than 10 percent of these youths can be classified as either drug abusing (defined as lacking control over the frequency and timing of drug consumption) or drug dependent—a designation based on a combination of factors, including age, type of drug used, family history and biochemistry, and exposure to negative consequences (e.g., legal penalties, loss of income, family conflict).[2]

Rates of substance abuse among youths referred to juvenile drug courts may well be higher than in the general population. For example, more than half of the juveniles taken into custody in 1999 had detectable traces of illicit drugs in urinalyses and other physical tests administered at the time of arrest.[3] But a positive test does not necessarily mean that an arrestee abuses or depends on drugs. Furthermore, research relying on clinical interviews to assess the extent of substance use disorders among juvenile offenders has produced inconsistent findings—depending on the study subjects (e.g., whether or not they were detainees, were randomly selected, or were from urban areas).

The extent of the difference between the drug problems of youths in general and those of juvenile drug court clients depends on the screening and assessment policies used in each program. If jurisdictions view their mission broadly—to deliver prevention services to as many alcohol- or drug-involved offenders as possible, regardless of the type of substance used or the severity of the problem—then the prevalence rate of abuse and dependence among youths enrolled in juvenile drug courts will be relatively low, as it is in the general population. A more narrowly focused mission to help teenagers who abuse serious and harmful drugs would boost that rate and indicate that those most imperiled were getting the help they need.

According to NEJDC researchers, juvenile drug courts must distinguish youths who are likely to become drug dependent from the majority of adolescent users who have experimented with alcohol or drugs but will not experience long-term problems as a result. Researchers found that only 10 to 20 percent of juveniles enrolled in the six drug courts under review had tried anything other than alcohol or marijuana. They concluded that programs are not focusing treatment resources on those whom they are intended to serve—adolescents least able to control their drug consumption and most at risk of prolonged and harmful substance abuse—and that courts are not yet clear about their purpose.

Entry into the drug court program

From a scientific or health perspective, the relevant criteria for determining when a "drug problem" exists are whether specific underlying drug use patterns can be (1) clearly defined and measured and (2) causally linked to negative or unhealthy outcomes. Most screening and assessment tools have been developed for adult populations and cannot be suitably adapted for use with adolescents. The Center for Substance Abuse Treatment has recommended several instruments for use in the juvenile justice system, including

the Substance Abuse Subtle Screening Inventory (SASSI), the Global Assessment of Individual Needs (GAIN), the Massachusetts Youth Screening Instrument (MAYSI), and the Comprehensive Addiction Severity Index for Adolescents (CASI–A).[4,5]

SASSI and MAYSI are screening tools that identify potential problems and indicate whether a more indepth assessment is needed in any area, such as mental health. CASI–A is both a screening and an assessment tool: it assesses the level of drug dependence and screens for other problems. CASI–A and GAIN, an assessment instrument, can be used as the basis for planning drug abuse treatment services.

Drug courts need to ensure that the screening and assessment tools they select are calibrated to match the characteristics—such as age, sex, and race/ethnicity—of the drug court population and that staff are trained to administer them properly, score them accurately, and interpret them correctly. For various reasons, including limited resources, many programs choose to assess client needs more informally, using self-reported information. While such data can be useful, using multiple sources of information ensures the most complete profile possible.

Age-appropriate interventions

Interventions for drug-involved juvenile offenders should account for the developmental status of individual youths. Adolescence is a period of physical, emotional, intellectual, and social change that often includes some rebelliousness and experimentation with high-risk behaviors, such as the use of illicit substances (see

ADOLESCENT DEVELOPMENT

Adolescent development falls into three phases, each characterized by different needs.

■ **Early adolescence** (between ages 10 and 14), when puberty occurs, may be the most difficult time for youths and the point at which they are likely to be most defiant. Early adolescence is marked by extreme self-consciousness, self-criticism, and dependence on peer acceptance and approval. These youngsters are especially sensitive to any disruptions, such as a change of school. Adolescents' growing attachment to peers combined with their desire for autonomy from parents can increase the risk of group-oriented problem behavior, including substance abuse and delinquency.

■ In **middle adolescence** (between ages 14 and 17), youths begin to feel more self assured, experiment more with image, have well-developed values and a variety of interests, resolve issues of identity and sexuality, and focus more on performance and achievement. A growing interest in and awareness of their own experiences and perceptions could increase curiosity about drugs and alcohol.

■ In **late adolescence** (between ages 17 and 20), youths become increasingly involved with the world outside home and school, begin the transition from social and financial dependence on family, have more stable relationships, and see themselves as adults. Although they are more focused on work and careers, the rates of illegal behavior (including substance use) peak during this time. College—known often to be a time of high alcohol and drug use—may, in effect, extend adolescence into the early twenties.

"Adolescent Development"). An awareness of the variations in adolescent development is essential for juvenile drug court practitioners, who must gauge the attractiveness of drugs to young offenders, provide treatment and services designed to change chronic or life-threatening drug-using behavior, and impose appropriate sanctions for noncompliance with program requirements.

Drug court personnel are most successful with younger adolescents when conversations are clear, open, and frank because many troubled young people have poor relationships with adults, limited life experience, little ability to deal with abstractions, and usually learn best from direct experience. Researchers stress that the courtroom process should be short, easy to understand, and free of legal or medical jargon. The first appearance in court should occur soon after the precipitating offense because adolescents are likely to discount the negative effects of delayed consequences.

Researchers note that most treatment models are developed for adults with more severe drug problems than youths. Some approaches used in adult treatment programs may transfer well to adolescent populations, but others may be unsuitable. For example, the Substance Abuse and Mental Health Services Administration recommends against using adult-style relapse prevention methods (i.e., cognitive-behavioral therapy (CBT)) techniques) that require the ability to imagine possible consequences of behavior and draw on past experience in ways that adolescents may be unable to do. In addition, the social isolation used in CBT as a response to relapse may be damaging to young offenders.[6]

Most treatment services are provided to youths in peer group sessions that are held on the treatment program's premises. Treatment practitioners note the need for very structured programming with clearly specified expectations and staff with strong group management skills to keep young offenders on task.

Child development specialists describe adolescence as a continuum, each new phase building on the last, with multiple alternate pathways available to each individual. The path taken is determined by various factors, including individual characteristics (e.g., language ability, knowledge, experience, and culture) and environmental constraints and opportunities. Social disadvantages, such as poverty, can affect progress. Youths in economically disadvantaged communities may have to assume adult responsibilities earlier than most young people, moving almost directly from childhood to adulthood. Researchers suggest that drug court personnel consider these social and contextual issues, as well as age and corresponding developmental stage, in working with juvenile substance abusers.

Juvenile offenders with frequent infractions often are placed in detention, which may expose them to harmful influences, causing additional problems. The appropriateness of detention must always be considered.

Juvenile drug court effectiveness

Juvenile drug courts have developed so rapidly that evaluators have not had time to complete studies with the long-term outcomes that are needed to demonstrate their effectiveness. Are drug courts better than the traditional juvenile justice system at stopping or reducing substance abuse in teenage offenders? How serious should a youth's drug behavior be to justify the added expense and treatment intensity of juvenile drug court? What happens to

juvenile offenders after they leave the drug court program? Researchers involved in the NEJDC project raise these and other critical questions, but until a body of sound evidence can be compiled, no definitive answers are forthcoming.

In the interim, the study team argues for stricter targeting policies, accurate and unbiased assessment and diagnosis practices, and treatment interventions that are informed by an understanding of adolescent development. To ensure that juvenile drug courts are cost effective and socially responsible, treatment needs to be focused on those youths with the most serious drug problems.

Notes

1. Butts, Jeffrey A., and John Roman, eds., *Juvenile Drug Courts and Teen Substance Abuse,* Washington, DC: The Urban Institute Press, 2004.

Under grant number 2000–DC–VX–K003, NIJ provided support to the Urban Institute for the National Evaluation of Juvenile Drug Courts project. The series of reports that resulted is based on examination of the procedures used in six NIJ-selected sites (juvenile drug courts in Charleston, South Carolina; Dayton, Ohio; Jersey City, New Jersey; Las Cruces, New Mexico; Missoula, Montana; and Orlando, Florida) and led to the development of a conceptual framework for evaluating juvenile drug courts.

2. Substance Abuse and Mental Health Services Administration, *Summary of National Findings, Vol. 1 of Results From the 2002 National Survey on Drug Use and Health,* NHSDA Series H–22, DHHS Publication No. SMA 03–3836, Rockville, MD: U.S. Department of Health and Human Services, Substance Abuse and Mental Health Services Administration, 2003.

3. National Institute of Justice, *1999 Annual Report on Drug Use Among Adult and Juvenile Arrestees,* Washington, DC: U.S. Department of Justice, Office of Justice Programs, National Institute of Justice, 2000. This document is available online at www.ncjrs.org/pdffiles1/nij/181426.pdf.

4. Winters, Ken C., *Screening and Assessing Adolescents for Substance Use Disorders,* Treatment Improvement Protocol (TIP) 31, Rockville, MD: Substance Abuse and Mental Health Services Administration, Center for Substance Abuse Treatment, 1999.

5. Winters, Ken C., William W. Latimer, and Randy D. Stinchfield. "Assessing Adolescent Substance Use." In *Innovations in Adolescent Substance Abuse Interventions,* ed. Eric Wagner and Holly B. Waldron, New York: Elsevier, 2001: 1–29.

6. Substance Abuse and Mental Health Services Administration, *Substance Abusing Adolescents,* Issues in Brief Series, Washington, DC: U.S. Department of Health and Human Services, Substance Abuse and Mental Health Services Administration, Center for Substance Abuse Treatment, Office of Policy Coordination, 1998.

Cost-Benefit Analysis of a Mature ☐ Drug Court

A cost-benefit evaluation of Portland, Oregon's Multnomah County Drug Court, the second oldest in the country, found that the drug court cost taxpayers significantly less than "business as usual."[1] The study also found that less intensive methods than those required for a formal cost-benefit analysis can be nearly as accurate in estimating costs, but much less expensive and time consuming.

Total savings from drug court participation over the 30-month study period—i.e., costs for drug court participants subtracted from costs for the comparison group— were more than $5,000 per participant. With the court's average annual caseload of 300, that amounts to more than $1.5 million per year.

The analysis focused exclusively on costs and benefits (or avoided costs) to taxpayers, examining three types:

- ■☐Investment costs (actual costs of using public resources, such as a judge's time, an attorney's time, law enforcement time, drug tests).

- ■☐Benefits from avoided system costs (criminal justice costs that would have been incurred as a result of rearrest if the drug court participant had not received treatment).

- ■☐Avoided victimization costs (lost days of work and medical expenses).

The total savings per drug court participant amounted to approximately $1,400 in investment costs, $2,300 in avoided court and law enforcement costs, and $1,300 in avoided victimization costs. (For details of the study method, see "Calculating the Cost Comparison.")

The need for cost-benefit data

The relationship between substance abuse and criminal activity is strongly supported by research. In 2000, almost two-thirds of arrestees had been involved with drugs before they were booked.[2] Strong evidence that drug abuse treatment reduces criminal behavior also exists. A recent congressionally mandated study found significant declines in criminal activity 12 months after treatment compared to the 12 months preceding it.[3] Evidence of the drugs-crime nexus, combined with the flood of drug offenders into the criminal justice system starting in the mid-1980s, was the impetus for seeking a solution that would break the cycle of arrest, incarceration, and rearrest. Drug courts—part of the movement toward "community courts"—were an attempt to do so through a court-based regimen of graduated sanctions and treatment and the avoidance of incarceration for minor offenses.

Research has shown that drug courts are effective in reducing criminal activity for offenders who complete the program. They also relieve courts of the congestion caused by the large number of drug-related cases. But the cost-effectiveness

CALCULATING THE COST COMPARISON

To compare the cost of drug court processing with standard processing of drug offenses, researchers calculated the costs of both types of cases. They also developed a less resource-intensive way of calculating costs.

The Sample

The overall sample consisted of 1,167 people, of whom about half were assigned to drug court and half to a "business as usual" comparison group that would be processed the standard way. From this overall sample, researchers selected 120 people—some from the drug court group and some from the comparison group—for intensive study and then recorded and timed all of their encounters with criminal justice and other agencies for a period of 30 months, to obtain accurate records of the time and cost of each transaction.

Because precise statistical analysis required more than 120 cases, data from the intensively studied subgroup were supplemented by administrative information from a larger sample. For example, the average length and cost of each transaction determined for the subgroup was combined with information on the number of transactions from the larger sample. By combining the data in this way, researchers could calculate the savings and costs for the larger group without following all 1,167 individuals.

An Easier Way

Researchers also tried to develop an easier, less resource-intensive way to calculate costs accurately by using readily available proxy data (estimates that can substitute for actual costs). For example, the total amount spent on arrest and booking can be divided by the number of arrests to determine a per-arrest cost. Proxy data from the administrative records of the larger sample were compared with actual costs tracked for the subgroup of 120 to determine if the proxy data could be used in future cost studies.

of drug courts has been difficult to determine. Identifying and calculating costs that involve multiple systems—the courts, corrections, and treatment—is a complex undertaking. The extensive involvement of drug courts in treatment was known to be costly, raising questions about whether the outcomes warrant the expense.

The evaluation of the Multnomah County Drug Court was conducted to help fill this gap in knowledge by assessing the court's costs and benefits over a 30-month period. Because a true cost-benefit evaluation is difficult to conduct, the study also tested the effectiveness of less time-consuming and less expensive estimation methods.

Drug courts save money and avoid costs

The research attempted to answer seven questions of interest to policymakers.

What is the total cost of the drug court for graduates and participants?

The total amount invested per person assigned to the drug court, including those who were terminated from the program early, averaged $5,928. This figure includes costs of the original arrest and booking, drug court hearings, drug court treatment, non-drug court treatment following termination, jail time, sanctions, and probation

costs for those terminated. The biggest expense was drug court treatment ($2,200); however, the per-day cost was far lower for treatment provided by the drug court than for treatment outside the drug court ($6.50 per day compared to $32 per day), suggesting that drug court treatment is a better long-term option. The next largest expense was jail time for those who were terminated—further evidence that drug court treatment is a less expensive option. The total annual cost for 300 drug court participants was $1.8 million, compared to $2.2 million for people in the "business as usual" group.

What are the investment costs of drug court compared with "business as usual"?

The costs of drug court time and "business as usual" court time are approximately equal. (Even though drug court requires more hearings than the "business as usual" process, drug court hearings take less time and require less preparation by the attorneys and the judge.) Treatment adds about $635 per participant to the cost of drug court.

The cost of jail and probation time for "business as usual" adds about $2,080 per participant. In all, drug court saves taxpayers approximately $1,442 per participant. (See exhibit 2 for a comparison of costs by type of transaction.)

What are the costs for each agency involved in drug court?

Costs are not borne equally by the different criminal justice agencies. The highest costs were for drug treatment and law enforcement (arrest, booking, and jail time). For law enforcement agencies, the highest cost was jail time for terminated drug court participants. Costs of the court, district attorney, and public defender were small, totaling about $500 per drug court client.

Exhibit 2. **Difference in investment costs: drug court vs. business-as-usual processing, by type of transaction**

Transaction	Drug Court Cost per Participant ($n = 594$)	Business-as-Usual Cost per Participant ($n = 573$)	Cost Difference
Arrest	$ 193	$ 193	$ 0
Booking	284	284	0
Court time	682	679	3
Treatment	2,644	2,009	635*
Jail time	1,611	2,783	-1,172*
Probation time	514	1,422	-908*
Total Cost	**$5,928**	**$7,370**	**-$1,442**

Note: Numbers have been rounded.
* Difference is significant at $p < .05$.

What are the benefits of drug court compared with "business as usual"?

Benefits were defined as the avoidance of law enforcement costs (prearrest, booking, jail time, and probation), court costs stemming from rearrest, and victimization costs (such as lost productivity and medical expenses). Drug court participants avoided an average of $2,329 in rearrest costs (including both law enforcement and court costs) and an average of $1,301 in victimization costs, for a total of $3,630 per participant over 30 months; overall, the program avoided a total of nearly $1.1 million per year. The biggest saving was in the cost of jail time avoided.

What are the benefits for each agency involved in the drug court?

Not surprisingly, the largest expense avoided was for law enforcement processing. Total avoided costs amounted to about $1,900 per participant; that is, it cost $1,900 more for law enforcement agencies to handle participants in the "business as usual" group. Costs avoided by other agencies were much less, ranging from $7 to $240 per participant.

Do some offices/agencies (e.g., district attorney, public defender) never recover their costs?

Over the course of the 30-month study, the court, the district attorney, and the drug treatment agency did not recoup their investments. However, the monetary losses to the court and the district attorney ($18 and $39, respectively, per drug court participant) were small and probably would eventually be recovered. Overall, the savings to Multnomah County of more than $1.5 million per year (a figure that includes lower investment costs, court and law enforcement costs avoided, and victimization costs avoided) represents a significant benefit to the taxpayer.

Can costs and benefits be measured more easily?

To find a simpler, less expensive way of calculating costs than the method used in a full-blown cost-benefit analysis, researchers identified sources that might substitute for the intensive study of participants. They compared data from the initial study (variables such as cost and length of encounters) with data obtained by reviewing administrative records and getting estimates from key informants such as judges and attorneys. In all cases, researchers found that administrative records were a reasonable proxy. Although the data were not as accurate as those obtained from the more intensive method, the figures were close, and the research resources invested were so much less that the proxies appear to be a more practical option for future studies.

The bottom line

Findings from the study of the Multnomah County Drug Court suggest that significant savings for taxpayers—primarily from reduced jail and probation time—can be achieved by using drug courts as an alternative to incarceration for drug-involved offenders. The cost for treatment provided via drug court, although high, is less than costs for treatment obtained elsewhere, e.g., as a condition of probation. In the long run, savings for law enforcement can be expected to more than compensate for treatment costs. However, costs and

savings may vary in other jurisdictions depending on the type of treatment provided and the characteristics of the drug court-eligible population, among other variables. Additional research is needed to answer the many questions that remain about the costs and benefits of drug courts.

Notes

1. This chapter is based on a report by Shannon M. Carey and Michael W. Finigan, "Detailed Cost Analysis in a Mature Drug Court Setting: A Cost-Benefit Evaluation of the Multnomah County Drug Court," prepared under grant number 2000–DC–VX–K004, which was awarded by NIJ to NPC Research, Inc. Available online at www.ncjrs.org/pdffiles1/nij/grants/203558.pdf.

2. National Institute of Justice, *2000 Arrestee Drug Abuse Monitoring: Annual Report,* Washington, DC: U.S. Department of Justice, Office of Justice Programs, National Institute of Justice, 2003 (NCJ 193013).

3. Center for Substance Abuse Treatment, *NTIES: The National Treatment Improvement Evaluation Study—Final Report,* Washington, DC: U.S. Department of Health and Human Services, Substance Abuse and Mental Health Services Administration, Center for Substance Abuse Treatment, March 1997. The National Treatment Improvement Evaluation Study, one of the largest studies of substance abuse treatment ever conducted, took place over a period of 5 years between 1992 and 1997 and involved more than 4,000 people who were being treated for drug and alcohol abuse.

About the National Institute of Justice

NIJ is the research, development, and evaluation agency of the U.S. Department of Justice. NIJ's mission is to advance scientific research, development, and evaluation to enhance the administration of justice and public safety. NIJ's principal authorities are derived from the Omnibus Crime Control and Safe Streets Act of 1968, as amended (see 42 U.S.C. §§ 3721–3723).

The NIJ Director is appointed by the President and confirmed by the Senate. The Director establishes the Institute's objectives, guided by the priorities of the Office of Justice Programs, the U.S. Department of Justice, and the needs of the field. The Institute actively solicits the views of criminal justice and other professionals and researchers to inform its search for the knowledge and tools to guide policy and practice.

Strategic Goals

NIJ has seven strategic goals grouped into three categories:

Creating relevant knowledge and tools

1. Partner with State and local practitioners and policymakers to identify social science research and technology needs.
2. Create scientific, relevant, and reliable knowledge—with a particular emphasis on terrorism, violent crime, drugs and crime, cost-effectiveness, and community-based efforts—to enhance the administration of justice and public safety.
3. Develop affordable and effective tools and technologies to enhance the administration of justice and public safety.

Dissemination

4. Disseminate relevant knowledge and information to practitioners and policymakers in an understandable, timely, and concise manner.
5. Act as an honest broker to identify the information, tools, and technologies that respond to the needs of stakeholders.

Agency management

6. Practice fairness and openness in the research and development process.
7. Ensure professionalism, excellence, accountability, cost-effectiveness, and integrity in the management and conduct of NIJ activities and programs.

Program Areas

In addressing these strategic challenges, the Institute is involved in the following program areas: crime control and prevention, including policing; drugs and crime; justice systems and offender behavior, including corrections; violence and victimization; communications and information technologies; critical incident response; investigative and forensic sciences, including DNA; less-than-lethal technologies; officer protection; education and training technologies; testing and standards; technology assistance to law enforcement and corrections agencies; field testing of promising programs; and international crime control.

In addition to sponsoring research and development and technology assistance, NIJ evaluates programs, policies, and technologies. NIJ communicates its research and evaluation findings through conferences and print and electronic media.

To find out more about the National Institute of Justice, please visit:

http://www.ojp.usdoj.gov/nij

or contact:

National Criminal Justice
 Reference Service
P.O. Box 6000
Rockville, MD 20849–6000
800–851–3420
e-mail: *askncjrs@ncjrs.org*

NCJ 211081

JUNE 06

MAILING LABEL AREA (5" x 2")

DO NOT PRINT THIS AREA

(INK NOR VARNISH)

www.ingramcontent.com/pod-product-compliance
Lightning Source LLC
Chambersburg PA
CBHW081240170526
45165CB00009B/3125